# Fishing with Pop

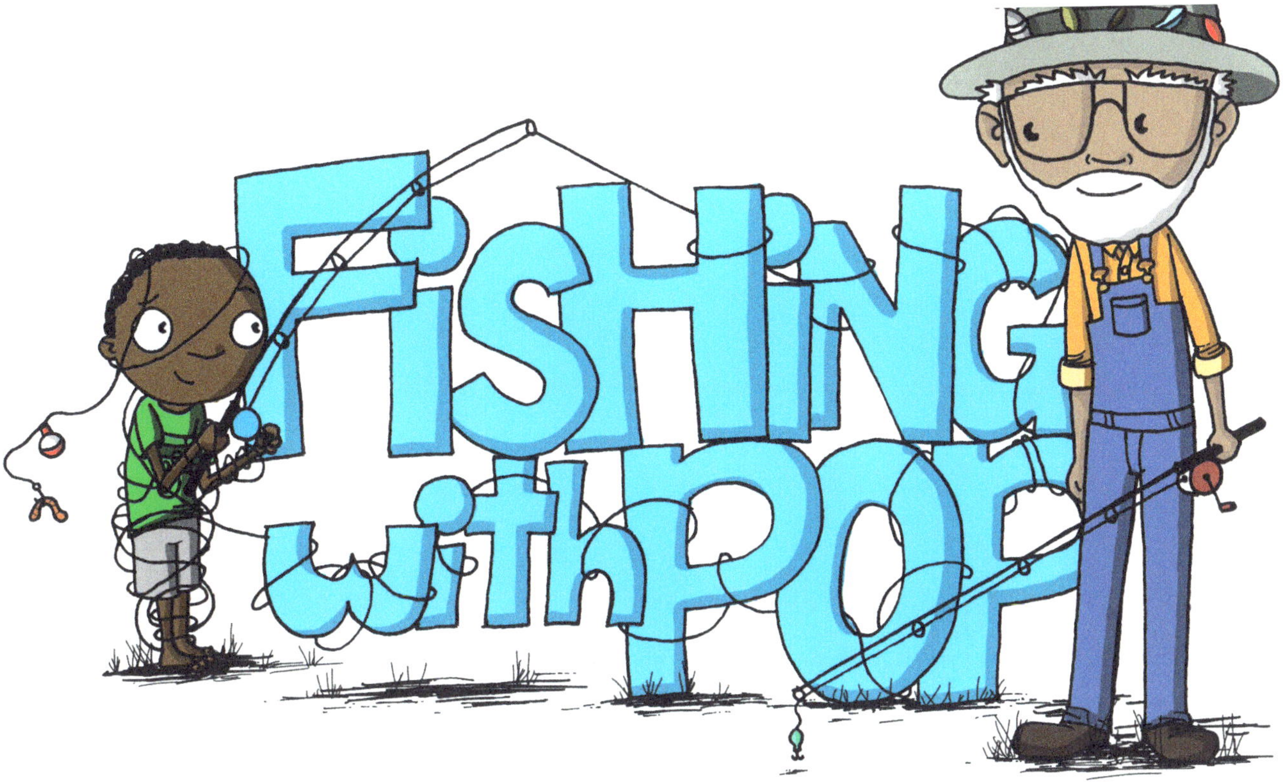

*Get hooked on reading!*
*Kelly*

**written by Chuck & Kelly Greenawalt**

**illustrated by Thomas Park**

*CATCH A BIG ONE!*
*— THOMAS*

www.lemonstarfish.com

Fishing With Pop

Copyright ©2016 by Chuck Greenawalt and Kelly Greenawalt

Illustrations ©2016 by Thomas Park

All rights reserved. This book or any portion thereof may not be reproduced or used in any manner whatsoever without the express written permission of the publisher except for the use of brief quotations in a book review.

Printed in the United States of America by Lemon Starfish
www.lemonstarfish.com

ISBN-10: 1-943806-10-1
ISBN-13: 978-1-943806-10-2

Library of Congress Control Number: 2015953265

The text of this book is set in 30 pt Dimbo font.
The illustrations in this book were created using Adobe Photoshop

For my creatures  - Thomas Park

For Pawpaw Lonnie and Grandpa Tommy  - C.G. & K.G.

My Pop has gray hair,
And a bushy beard.
He talks real loud,
And he smells real weird.

He kisses Grandma and calls her honey.

He watches football,
He shows me things...

He even shares
His chicken wings.

Today I plan
To find out where
My pop is at when
He's not in his chair.

"Where are you going, Pop?
What is that?"
"I'm off to the lake,
It's my fishin' hat."

"Can I come too, Pop?
That sounds like fun!"
"Grab your shoes, bud,
It's time to run."

I climb up in
My Pop's red jeep.
I press the horn,
It yells, "Beep! Beep!"

"You can't drive, bud,
Move on down!"
We pull out of the driveway,
And head away from town.

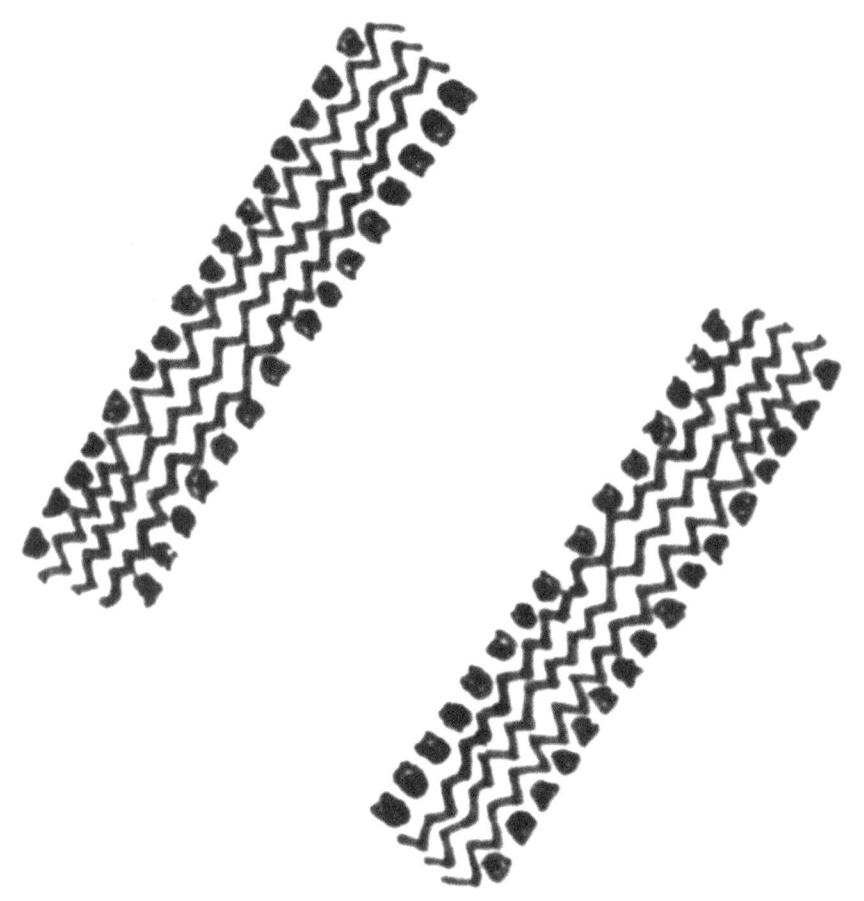

We drive and drive,
To the lake.
I try and try
To stay awake.

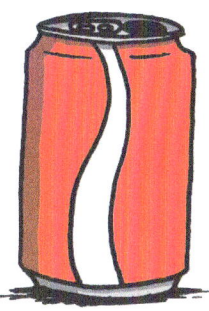

We park the jeep,
We grab the gear.
We walk to the water,
And he says, "Right here!"

"Pop! Pop! Pop!
I've caught a big one!"
"It's just a shoe,
Now try again, son."

Fishing seemed like
Lots of fun,
But I'm getting real tired
Of not catching one.

"Don't give up, bud,
The bass are bitin!'"
He reels one in
And it sure is fightin.'

Pop has skills,
That's for sure.
I wish I was using
His lucky lure.

I reel, reel, reel
With all my might.
I bring him in,
He's big, alright.

Pop gets the net,
And helps me out.
He gets so excited
That he starts to shout.

"Good job, bud!
That was great!"
We high five
And celebrate.

"It's time for lunch,
Grandma will be waiting.
There's no more time
For casting and baiting."

I climb in the jeep,
And we drive on back.
Don't tell Grandma,
But we stop for a snack.

CPSIA information can be obtained
at www.ICGtesting.com
Printed in the USA
FSOW03n0011040516
20008FS